Here
to Help

FIREFIGHTER

Rachel Blount

Photography by Bobby Humphrey

W
FRANKLIN WATTS
LONDON·SYDNEY

Franklin Watts
First published in Great Britain in 2015 by The Watts Publishing Group

Credits
Series Editors: Rachel Blount and Paul Humphrey
Series Designer: D. R. ink
Photographer: Bobby Humphrey
Produced for Franklin Watts by Discovery Books Ltd.

Dewey number: 363.3'7'092
HB ISBN: 978 1 4451 4000 1
Library ebook ISBN: 978 1 4451 4001 8

Printed in China

Franklin Watts
An imprint of
Hachette Children's Group
Part of The Watts Publishing Group
Carmelite House
50 Victoria Embankment
London EC4Y 0DZ

an Hachette UK company
www.hachette.co.uk

www.franklinwatts.co.uk

The publisher and packager would like to thank the following people for their help and involvement with the book: Leanne Player, Phil Major, all the members of Blue Watch at Hereford fire station and the crew at Kington Fire Station.

Contents

Words in **bold** are in the glossary on page 24.

I am a firefighter

My name is Leanne and I am a firefighter. It is my job to fight fires and rescue people who may be in trouble.

? Why do you think fire engines are red?

This is the fire station where I work. We have four fire engines here. We also have a boat, for river and **flood** rescues.

Brian
Watch commander

Meet Blue Watch, the **crew** I work with. My **watch commander**, Brian, is wearing a white helmet. He is the first person to find out about any **emergency calls**.

My uniform

At work I wear a **uniform**. The trousers are dark blue and I wear a red T-shirt and a dark blue shirt.

?

Why do firefighters wear a uniform when they do their job?

If we get an emergency call I put my fire **kit** and boots on as fast as I can. I wear a yellow helmet with a **safety visor**.

Helmet and visor

Breathing apparatus

Torch

Gloves

Fire-retardant jacket and trousers

300 BAR AIR

Hi-vis jacket

Boots

At the station

My shift starts at 9:00 am.

In we go.

First, I check the equipment on the fire engine. This is a pump. We use it to take water from rivers and lakes for fighting fires.

I check my breathing apparatus is working properly and has enough air for an emergency.

? Can you think of three ways that firefighters help us?

Emergency!

My **bleeper** goes off.
It's the commander.
There is an emergency!
A car has crashed into
a tree and someone is
trapped inside.

The crew and I run to the
engine. We get into our fire kit as
quickly as we can. Our trousers are rolled down
over our boots so we can put them on quickly.

We speed off to the scene of the accident. The driver turns on the lights and the **siren**. These warn other drivers to move aside to let us pass. On the way, Brian tells us what he wants us to do when we arrive.

Why are firefighters called to traffic accidents?

Keeping calm

We work with other **emergency services** at road accidents. When we arrive, we check with the **paramedics** for any other **casualties**.

The passenger stuck inside the car is injured, so we need to get him out quickly. I use the cutting tool to take the roof off the car.

I talk to the casualty to let him know what is happening and to keep him calm.

Don't worry, we're just taking off the roof.

?

Why do firefighters talk to people who are stuck in an emergency?

It doesn't take long for us to get him free. An ambulance takes him to hospital. Once we are sure that the area is safe, we return to the station.

Fighting fires

Back at the station, my bleeper goes again. The kitchen in a nearby restaurant is on fire! We have to move fast.

I use the stairs and then the pole to get to the fire engine quickly.

At the back of the restaurant, Paul and I put on our breathing apparatus.

Inside, it is full of smoke. We check every room.

?

What should you do if you see lots of smoke or flames coming from a building?

We use water to put the fire out and then we can return to the station.

Drills

When we are not attending emergencies we have **drills** to make sure we know the latest fire and safety **procedures**.

Today, Brian tells us we are doing a ladder drill.

We take the ladder from the roof of the fire engine...

... and set it up.

You can't be scared of heights when you are a firefighter.

It's a long way down!

? Have you ever been high up off the ground? How did it make you feel?

Working in the community

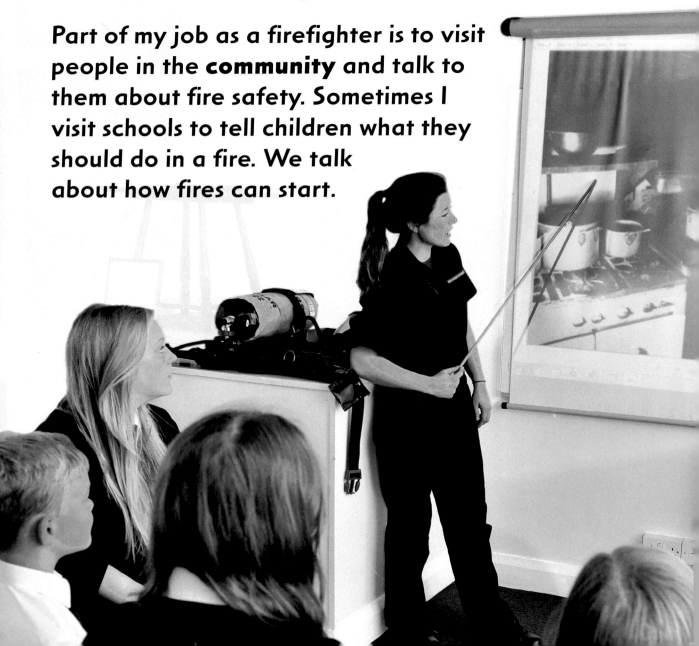

Part of my job as a firefighter is to visit people in the **community** and talk to them about fire safety. Sometimes I visit schools to tell children what they should do in a fire. We talk about how fires can start.

It is important to have smoke alarms fitted in your house. They beep very loudly when they **detect** smoke to warn you that there may be a fire.

?

Why is it important for firefighters to tell people about fire safety?

DON'T FORGET!

Check the battery in your smoke alarm

www.firekills.gov.uk

FIRE KILLS

The end of the day

At the fire station we work in shifts, so there is always someone ready to answer emergency calls 24 hours a day.

It is nearly 5:00 pm and the end of my shift, but there are still jobs to do. I fill up the engine's tank with **fuel** ready for the next emergency.

That's full now.

Why is it important that emergency calls can be answered 24 hours a day?

I help clean the fire engine.

Then it's time to go home.

Helping people

Each day can be very different as a firefighter. It can be dangerous, but I enjoy my job and most of all I enjoy helping people.

When you grow up...

If you would like to be a firefighter here are some simple tips and advice.

What kind of person are you?

- You are brave, fit and active
- You enjoy working as part of a team
- You are not afraid of heights or the dark
- You can keep calm and think clearly in an emergency
- You are confident and can communicate clearly
- Most of all, you enjoy helping people.

How do you become a firefighter?

You do not need any qualifications to become a firefighter, but you will need to pass a series of written, medical and fitness tests. Any qualifications you gain may help with your future in the service.

To find out more about the fire service visit: www.fireservice.co.uk

Answers

P5. Fire engines are red so they can be easily seen.

P6. Firefighters wear a uniform that is fire retardant so that when they get close to fire they are well protected.

P9. Firefighters help us in many ways; they help fight fires; they attend vehicle accidents; they can rescue people, or animals that might be stuck in floods.

P11. Firefighters are trained to deal with vehicle accidents. There is special equipment on fire engines to make sure vehicles and people who may be stuck inside them can be made safe as quickly as possible.

P13. Firefighters talk to people because it is important to keep an accident victim calm.

P15. Phone 999 and ask for the fire service. Try and make a note of where and when you saw the fire or smoke. Every bit of information will help the emergency services.

P19. Firefighters need to educate people about fire safety so that they know what to do in an emergency.

P20. Emergency calls must be answered 24 hours a day because emergencies can happen at any time of night or day.

Were your answers the same as the ones in this book? Don't worry if they were different, sometimes there is more than one right answer. Talk about your answer with other people. Can you explain why you think your answer is right?

Glossary

bleeper an electronic device that firefighters wear; it bleeps when they are needed in an emergency

breathing apparatus breathing equipment; firefighters wear a tank on their back and breathe air from it through a mask when they are in a smoke-filled building

casualties people that are hurt or injured

community a group of people who live in the same area

crew people with special skills who work together

detect discover

drill to train or exercise

emergency call when a member of the public calls 999 for emergency assistance

emergency services the police, fire and paramedics are all emergency services

fire retardant being able to slow the spread of fire

flood when an area is covered in deep water after heavy rain or when a river has burst its banks

fuel diesel or petrol that is used to power vehicles

hi-vis describes a material that is visible when it is dark

kit another name for a uniform and equipment

paramedics people who provide emergency care to sick or injured people and take them to hospital

procedures a series of actions that are done in a certain order

safety visor a clear mask worn to protect the face

shift a period of time when you are at work

siren a machine that makes a wailing noise to warn other road users that an emergency vehicle is near

uniform special clothing worn by people who belong to the same organisation

watch commander a senior firefighter who is in charge of the watch at a fire station

Index